6 Bin System Landscape

Organized and prioritized for life.

6 Bin System Landscape

Organized and prioritized for life.

Carl A. Beard

IN-CHARGE LLC

IN-CHARGE LLC

Pen In-Charge LLC
500 Paterson Plank Road #8004
Union City, New Jersey 07087
Hotline: (551) 414-2023

Ordering Information:

Special discounts are available on quantity purchases by corporations, associations, and others. For details, contact the publisher at the address above.

Printed in the United States of America.

ISBN-13:	Paperback:	978-1-972881-50-7
	eBook:	978-1-972881-51-4

Library of Congress Control Number: 2026919643

Dedication

To everyone who has a mound of paperwork on their desk.

FOREWORD

Hello and welcome to the world of super efficiency.

This resource came from a real-world story during my ten years as IT Manager at a manufacturing company in Los Angeles, CA.

Working as an IT manager and ISO coordinator, organization and efficiency have been a fascination with me.

The study of efficiency and synergistic flow of data came from my years at Moorpark Jr. College, graduating with an AA in Accounting and a BS in Business Management Information Systems. From CSUN.

Life is full of opportunities and this resource. happened to be one of them. I had known Ish for almost ten years before that fateful day. Working with him came naturally.

His resource is a culmination of over 40 years of manufacturing industry experience, working in the accounting, IT, and manufacturing industries.

Table of contents

Bibliography

The Brain From Top to Bottom
Internet May 2022
https://thebrain.mcgill.ca/flash/capsules/experience_jaune03.html

New King James Copyright by Nelson Publishing 2019

www:/Anthony Robbins/massive action.2023

Dale Carnegie, "How to Win Friends and Influence People," Simon and Schuster, 2010

GOAL

It is important that you succeed in reading and acting on this resource. So, think about and write down why you would be willing to create a 6-Bin system for yourself. The payoff and benefits are equally important. Al smart goals have a due date. When will you finish is just as important as when you will start. I encourage you to write me at cbeard@isosherpa.com when you complete your 6-Bin system.

Why are you doing this? ______________________

____

____

____

What is the payoff, and by when?

____

____

____

Chapter 1

From chaos to order

As the Information Systems Manager, I had gotten to know my fellow coworkers. The group I interacted with the most was the customer service representatives (CSRs). These were the employees who processed the most paperwork in the company. A steady flow of customers, requests for quotes (RFQs), Quotes, Sales Orders, and Customer Complaints was never-ending. Each person had their own way of dealing with the myriad of papers. Ish did not have a system, and his desk showed it.

I had a good relationship with Ish. He was one of the most active Customer Service Representatives. Ish had been with the company from day one and wanted to grow into the head CSR. He had good customer skills and knew the products very well. His one flaw was obvious. He had taken on too much, and his desk reflected his disorganization. Ish confided in me that he wanted to be the head CSR for the company. My first thought was, "Not with that desk." This particular Friday, I could hear the din of conversations in the sales room when the sales manager came in and quietly closed my office door. He explained that Ish wanted to be promoted to head CSR, but was so disorganized that he could not see it happening. I had to agree with him. As I looked up from my desk. I saw it in an instant. Six plastic, stackable bins floating in the air. The idea was powerful and clear. Now I would have a chance to execute it. Looking into the sales manager's anxious eyes, I responded, "Yes." It was possible. Could I spend some time with Ish, " I asked him?" Yes, was his enthusiastic reply. The challenge of helping Ish realize his dream was on. Excitement built in me as the thought of changing a person's life outcome settled in my consciousness.

I waited a few minutes after the sales manager had left my office. During this time, I drew the edifice that would change a person's life. It looked like six bins stacked on top of each other. This is the question I heard from the small still voice within me. "What are the five things you do that bring value to the company?" A simple but very powerful question. I had to admit. I even asked myself if I was doing the five things that brought value to the company. As I looked into the sales office, I saw that Ish had a desk chock-full of papers, rolls of adhesives, and samples. How was order going to be established from such chaos? Would he be willing to go through the transformation? Was I only the IT guy?

Was my connection based on a sense of friendship and respect with Ish? Would he trust me to guide him through such a monumental transformation? More importantly, would he stick with the 6-bin system or abandon it after the first week of use?

It was nearing the end of the day, and most of the other employees had left the office. I got up from my desk and slowly walked over to Ish. I had one question for him. "Hello, Ish", I said. How would you like to be the next head CSR? He leaned back in his chair and gave me a resounding "yes." I leaned forward with a smile and said, "Ish, I can help you with your dream. If you let me help you. Are you willing to try?" Ish sat in his chair for some time and then said: "Yes, let's do it."

Chapter 2

Transformation in six steps

I looked straight into Sih's eyes and said, "We need to clear your desk of all this clutter. He hesitated for a moment and agreed with my idea. I brought over a table we could use to offload the desk. We were methodical as we cleared the stacked papers, samples, quotes, orders, and other extraneous items. We kept at it until the desk was clean. We also cleared the drawers until they were empty. I then asked Ish the question I had heard before, in my office." Ish, what are the five things you do that add value to the company?" His reply," quotes, sales orders, customer service."

The company had just started an ISO initiative. I asked Ish. "What about your ISO duties?" We started writing down a list and would prioritize it once we were done. I noticed a bunch of samples and asked. "Are you in purchasing?" No, Ish responded. We cleared all the samples and extraneous materials into a round file or set them aside for the sample room.

As we stacked the pile of papers into corresponding Groups, I asked Ish. What is the top priority activity? He quickly responded with quotes. At this point, we put all the quotes in the first of the 6 bins. What is next on your list of priorities?" I asked. Sales orders, Ish replied. This stack also went into the first bin. Next on top of orders. Customer returns were third. Then came Requests for quotes (RFQs)s. Then the ISO quality documents came last. I moved a large trash can over, and we dumped all the other non-essential documents into it. Note: we did not empty the trash can yet. The next phase was to file each group in priority order. Ish decided that Request for quotes (RFQs) should go in bin 2. This was followed by quotes in Bin 3, sales orders in Bin 4, and customer complaints in Bin 5. Finally, in Bin 6, we slid in the ISO documents. Now it was time to explain to Ish that we had just prioritized and organized Sih's work. I explained that every other paper form and document that did not add value to his work was not relevant. Ish sat in silence for a few minutes. He was trying to take in what had just happened. Compared to the other CSRs' desks, his desk looked immaculate.

We revisited the trash can with the papers we had dumped. This was to make sure we had not overlooked any important documents. The round file was now ready to be emptied.

Chapter 3

The power of the 6-Bin system

It's one thing to organize your work, but another to strategically organize your workflow and prioritize it at the same time.

Once set up, any paper that landed in the number

1 In Bin could be immediately prioritized and organized into its corresponding In Bin. The workload could now be done from highest priority to lowest. The 6-Bin system takes the power of work prioritization and serves the human brain function to create a synergistic and efficient flow of work that adds value to the enterprise's value stream. Large food distribution chains such as McDonald's use this power by color coding machines and placing them in the same place throughout the chain of stores. You may be wondering why 6 and not seven or eight bins. Studies have shown that once a person has to memorize more than six items, the seventh falls off their synaptic memory list. Memory List research "The Brain from Top To Bottom"

One more factoid. The number of "Man" is six in the biblical reference. Revelation 13:18-New King James Version. Man was made to work in a framework of six. It also happens that 6 bins are high enough to organize work but not be unstable enough to topple over. Workflow was not constrained, and you could see over the 6-nin system.

It should be noted that stores sell bins in groups of five and also single bins. Metal, plastic, or wood bins work just as well.

Chapter 4

Ease of mind at all levels

Once we completed the 6-Bin exercise, I asked, how do you feel, Ish? His answer was "illuminating. Like a large weight has been lifted from my back." What Ish experienced was a mental release of the responsibility that all that clutter was creating for him. He was free at last. I explained to Ish that this is a powerful concept. I also explained the following. When he stepped away from his desk, the other CSRs could find any document in a flash. This would be an immediate improvement in customer service. I explained to him that when He went on vacation, he would have peace of mind that the department would run smoothly. The underlying power of the 6-Bin system was revealed. When the other employees came in on Monday, they had one question. "Who fired Ish?" I was on hand to announce a promotion, and not a demotion had transpired. Ish triumphantly walked to his desk and took his place as head CSR. Change is hard for anyone. Ish had transformed his workspace in a matter of hours. Then the positive comments started in. Wow, now we can find orders. This is great. Finally, the comment I was waiting for. Can we do this too? The transformation had begun. Our Customer Service Department was empowered to succeed. Better yet, there was genuine anticipation and excitement to use the new 6-Bin System. When a group of people decides to move in the same direction, it can create permanent change in the enterprise. The 6-Bin System transformed a whole department from chaos to a cohesive and synergistic customer service team.

Chapter 5

Duplication is Power

It was great that Ish had a 6-Bin system. But what about the other CSRs? Successful leaders lead by example. Carnegie wanted the benefit of 100 workers, not his own 100% effort. "How to win friends and influence people." Duplication is the most powerful workload advantage. During the first day, I spent time coaching Ish on the use of his 6-Bin system. This included organizing the other CSRs on the floor. Soon, Six Bin towers were popping up all over the place. As it happened, Ish did go on vacation, and the document flow continued to be smooth and efficient. During his vacation, one day I happened to walk by Sih's vacant desk. One of the CSRs asked if a customer request for a quote was at his desk?. Sure enough, in the blink of an eye, the request for quote was found and quoted. Now, all the CRS had witnessed and experienced the power of the 6-Bin system. The atmosphere in the sales room changed to one of empowerment.

Chapter 6

Making the 6 Bin system work for you.

Here is how you can transform your work area in a few steps.

Use the form below to write down the five activities that add value to your company. Here is a valuable tip. If you encounter more than six, write them down on a separate list. You may find that you are creating a 6-Bin for someone to delegate to. You may find that one of your 6-Bin priorities is being replaced by one on the list. DO NOT EXCEED 6 items. This is a rule that should not be broken under any circumstances. You will thank me later. Here are some questions I have been asked. Can I have more than one 6 Bins System? Yes, if you wear more than one hat. Remember, you have to manage each 6-Bin system. Can I change an item or rearrange the order? Yes. My direct reports have a different 6-Bin system. Yes, they add value Differently, than you do. Can my 6-Bin system be bilingual? Si Señor oh Señorita.

Step One

Get yourself 6 stackable bins. Yes, stackable works best. I noticed that Staples is selling wire stackable bins. This also works well and looks cool. Try to use the same type of bins in each department.

Label each bin using your organization list.

Step Two

Take all the papers in your office or desk and sort them by the 5 things that add value. Yes, that will mean that your desk area will be completely cleared off.

GET RID OF ALL EXTRANEOUS PAPERS, SAMPLES, RETURNS, ENGINEERING GADGETS, ETC. BE RUTHLESS, HAVE AN ASSISTANT HELP

Step Tree

Stack all your identified papers in your number one bin.

From your Number One bin file, each paper in its proper bin. This does a couple of things. It sets a standard of activity and muscle memory. And allows you to find and filter out any extraneous documents.

When you come in tomorrow, people should say Wow, does he still work here.

Step Four

Sit back and visualize your creation. Let it sink in. Remember, all those focus temptations will try to flood in and add to your system. Reject them.

Questions

6-Bin issues. What if the stack of papers does not fit? In my In-Bin Arbitrage, your stack. Go through the stack and sort by the following order.

New – Work in Progress – Completed

New goes into the Bin.

Work in progress gets acted on immediately or delegated.

Completed gets filed by you or an assistant.

You should find that you have about 5 to 10 documents to work on in each Bin.

Second 6-Bin Issue.

When I am away, how do I keep my bins from overflowing? Answer: assign someone to process that bin for you. This includes clearing the number 1-In bin to the 5 bins below.

Third 6-Bin Issue

What do I do with documents from my boss or other departments? Return the documents and negotiate with the source.

Why does it add value to the company? Why should you be doing it and not someone else? Remember, they may not know how the 6-Bin system works.

Fourth 6-Bin Issue

I am stuck and can't think of five things I do that add value to the company. Here is a simple mind map exercise that works every time. Draw a circle. Draw 5 lines from the circle. See the diagram below. On each line, write down one thing you do for the company based on your job

description. Write the action you do and the benefit it creates for the company. You will assign a priority value to each action. Your mind works in a circular fashion. So you can capture your creative thoughts on the mind map and place them on the 6-Bin worksheet below.

PRIORITY ACTIVITY BENEFIT

1	Process Orders	Generate Income
2	Stock Inventory	Add value to stock
3	Answer Phones	Customer Service
4	Order Status	Keep customers & shipping informed
5	Data Entry	Update order Status

This is called a mind map. See www:/mindmap

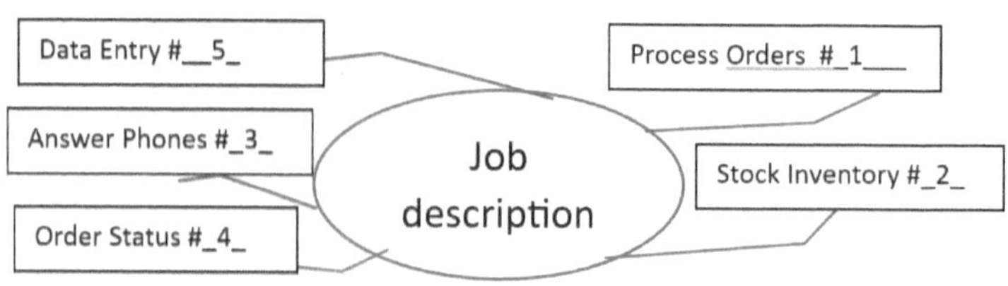

6 BIN WORKSHEET

WHAT ADDS VALUE Example-Quotes	*PRIORITIZE 2-6*	*WHO*	*DELEGATE*
IN BIN Start Here	*1*		
	2		
	3		
	4		
	5		
	6		

BE RUTHLESS -NO EXCEPTIONS-DELEGATE – DELEGATE - DELEGATE

Chapter 7

Duplicate the power, Multiply your success.

This system is catching. I got a discreet call from the accounting manager. Can you help one of my ladies? You have seen the Peanuts Character Pig Pen. You get the idea. The 6-Bin system spread throughout the company. Creating success at all levels of the enterprise. How did this affect me, you may ask? When it came time for my review, my raise of 30% was doable according to the CEO. Here is a tip: "Start Today." Anthony Robbins says, "Massive action creates massive change" www:/Anthony Robbins/massive action. Creating a 6-Bin system represents massive action in your life. I am confident that this resource will guide you on our path to an Organized and Prioritized for Life strategy. Called the 6-Bin System.

www.ingramcontent.com/pod-product-compliance
Lightning Source LLC
Chambersburg PA
CBHW031353230926
51848CB00002B/509
9781972881507